# Shark Coloring Book For Adults

## Sharks Coloring Book for Adults Relaxation containing 30 Shark designs for Sress Relief Coloring for Grown-ups

### Coloring Books For Adults: Vol 16

by The Coloring Book People

ISBN-13: 978-1544015156

ISBN-10: 1544015151

# Preview Page

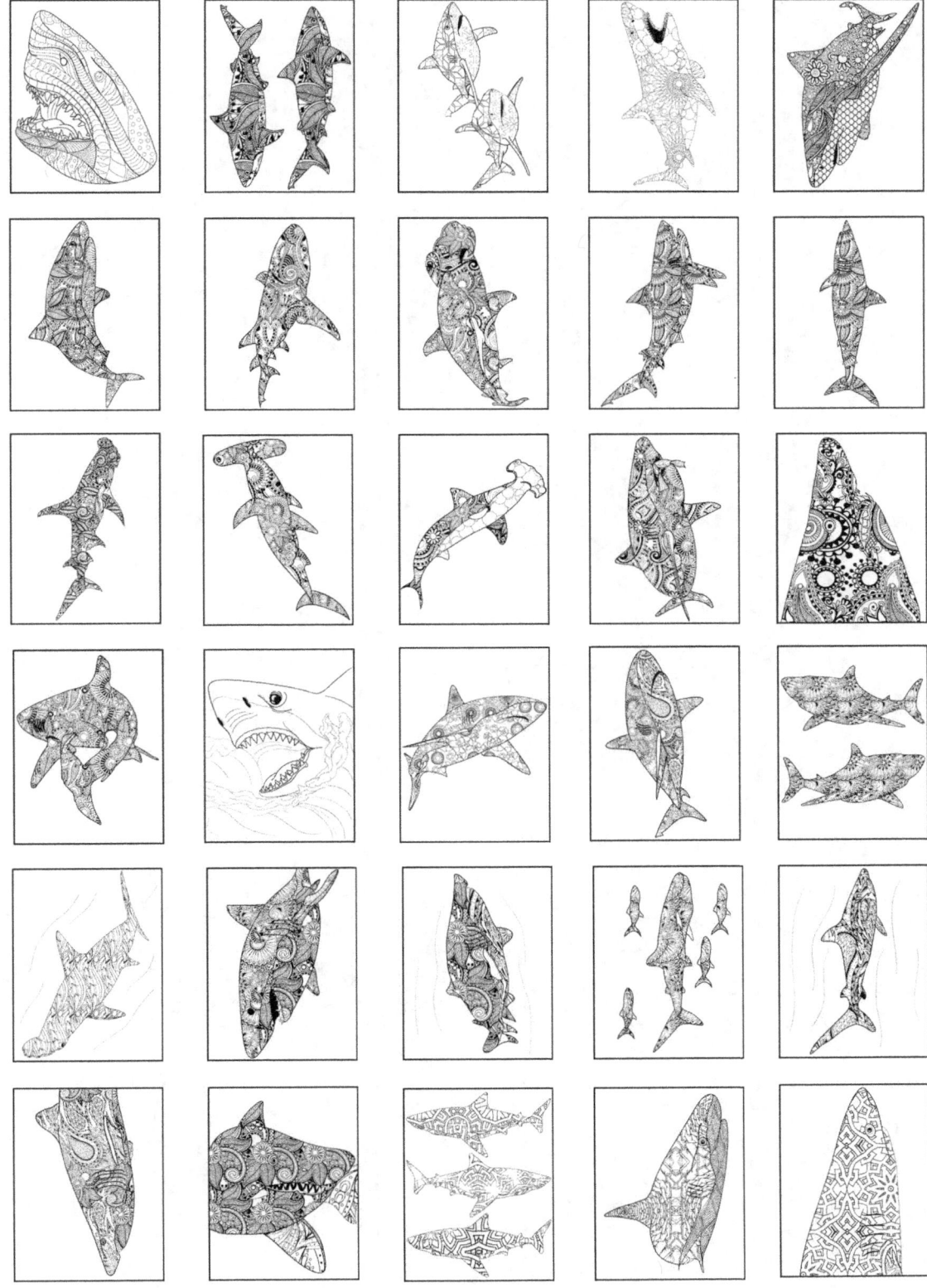

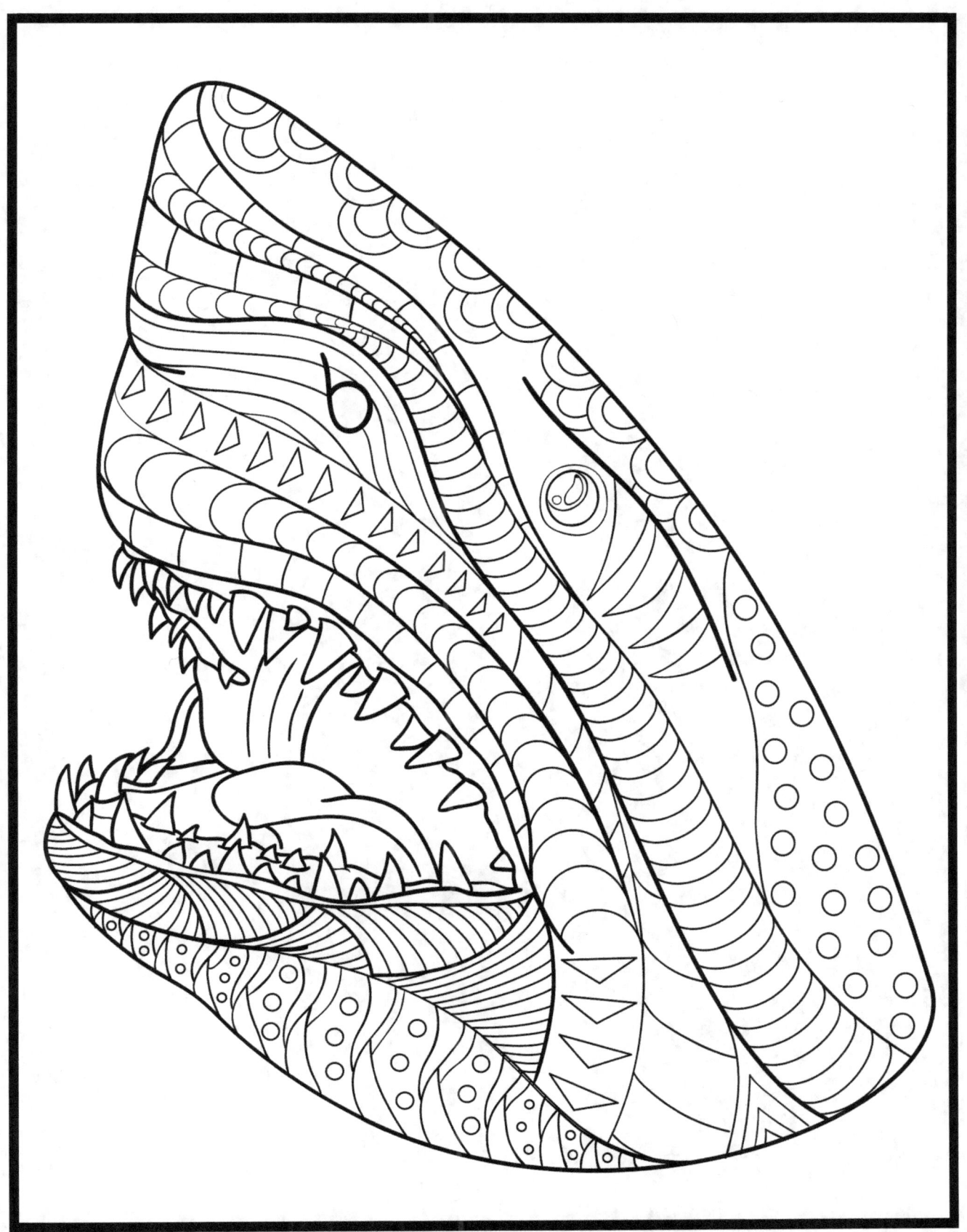

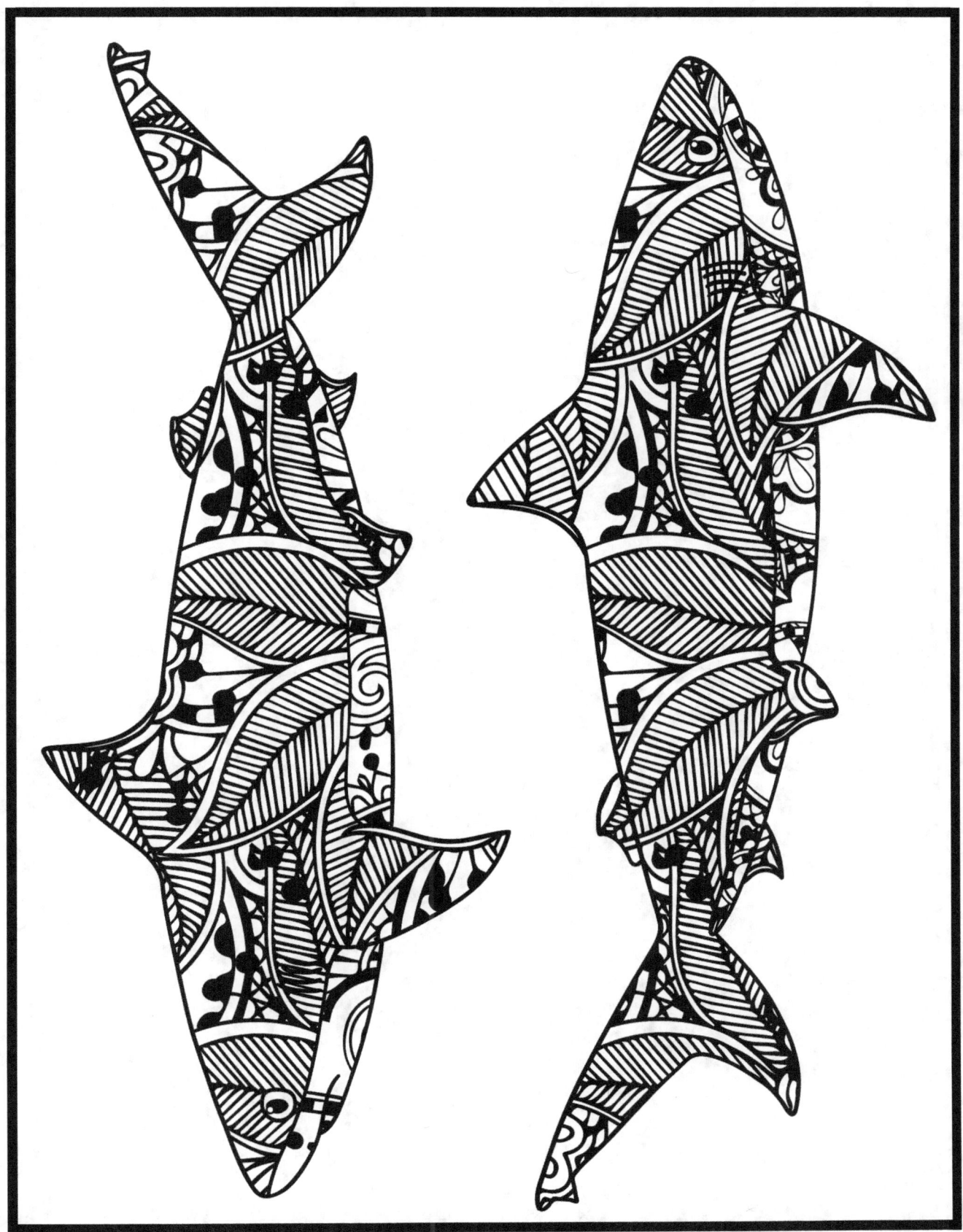

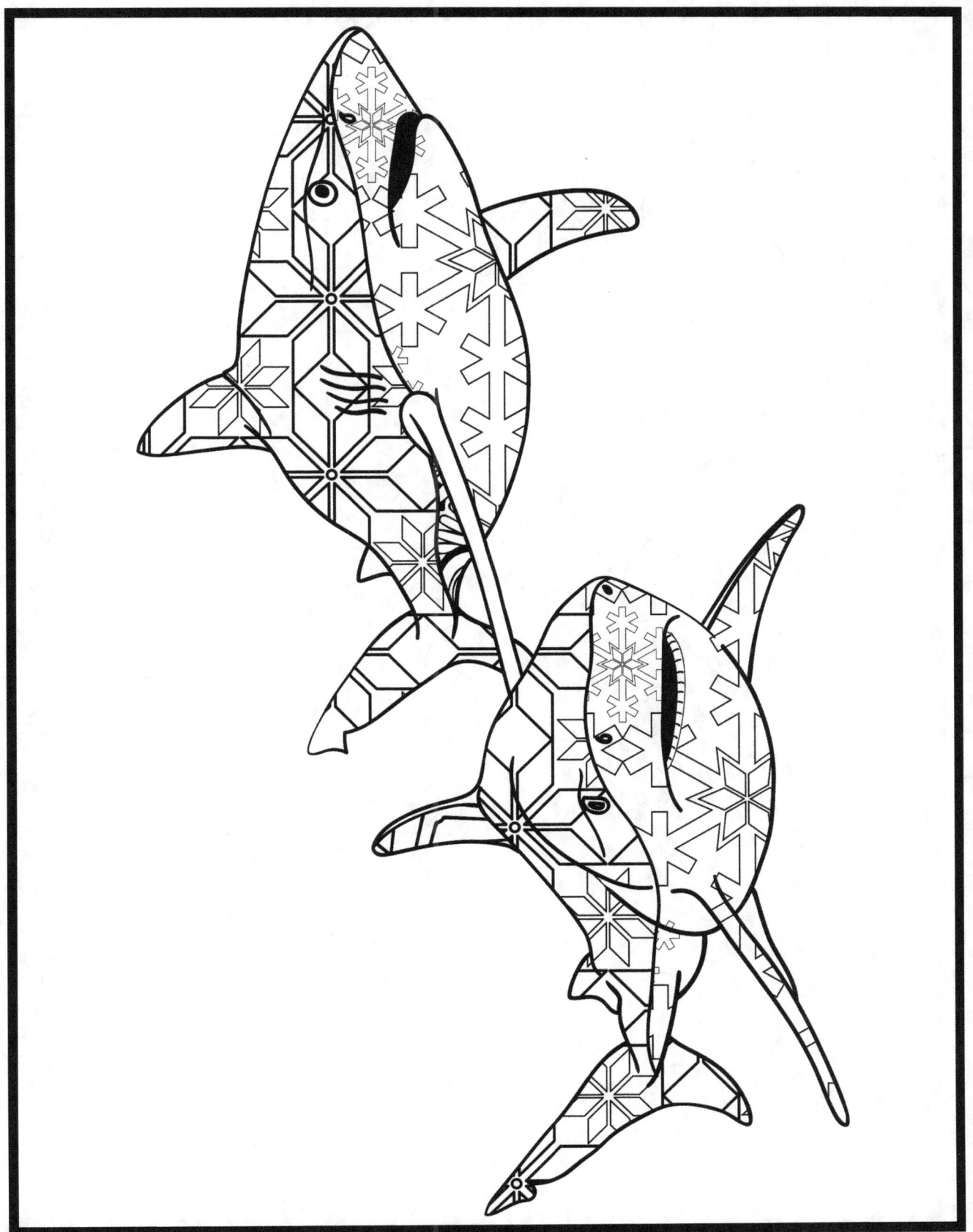

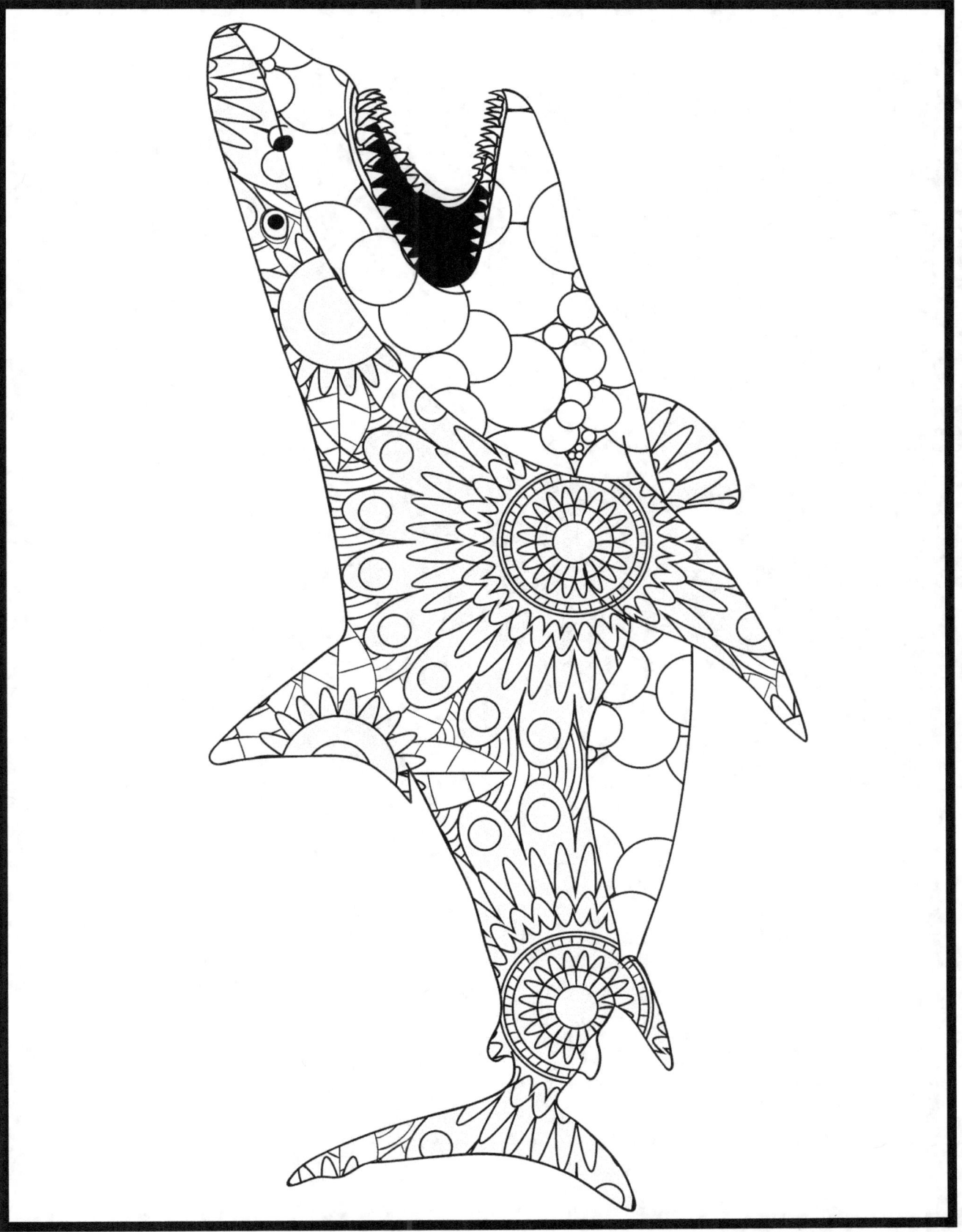

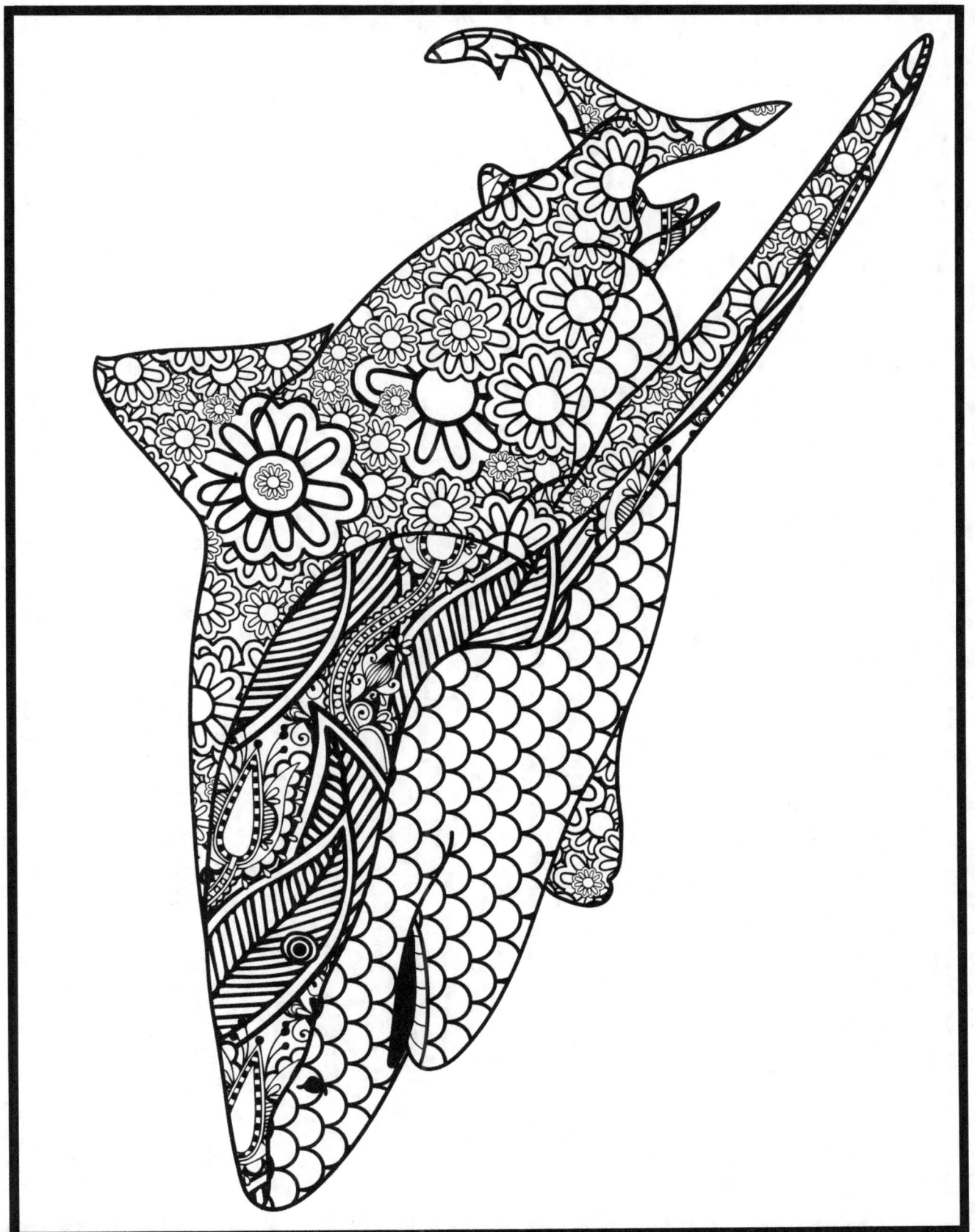

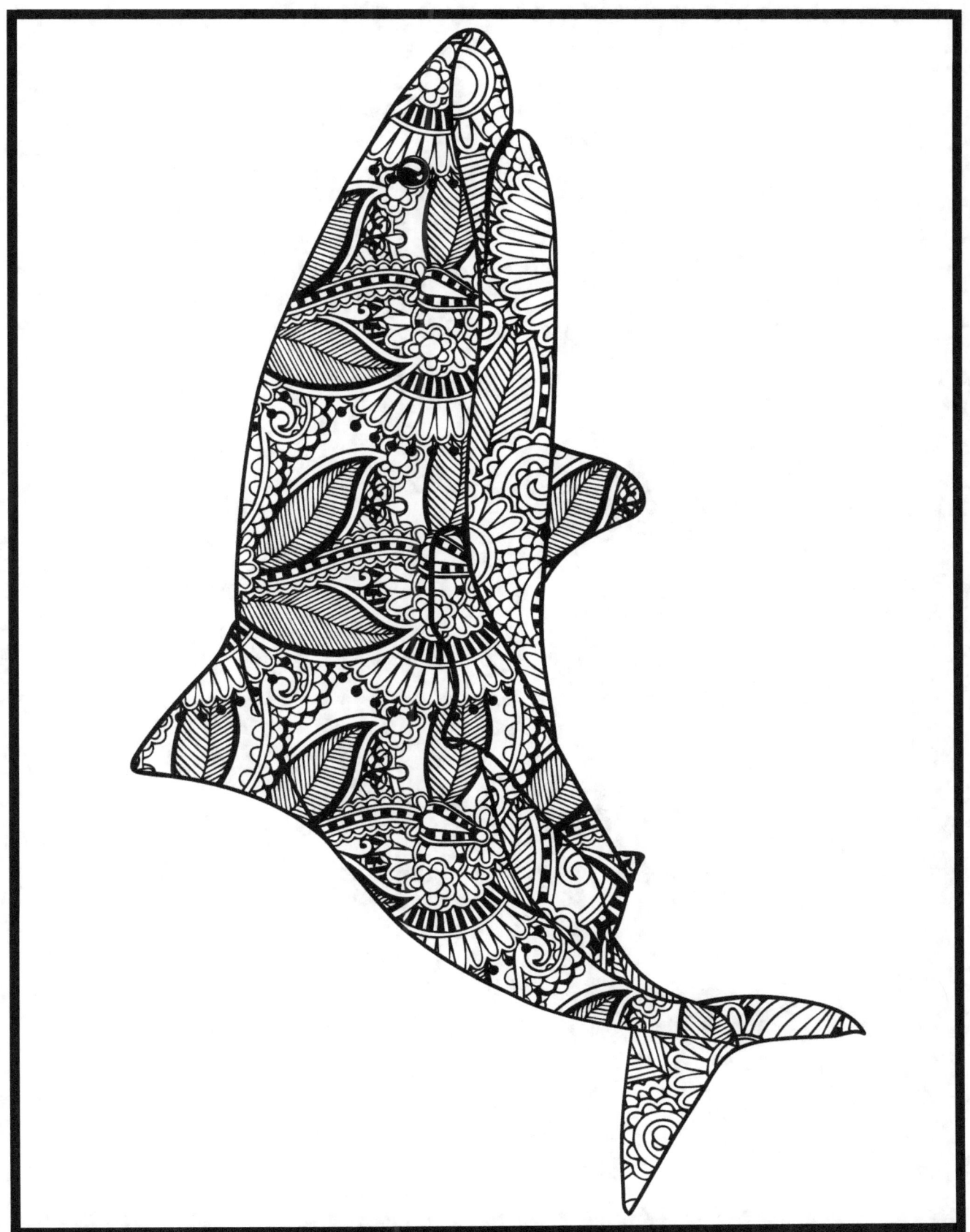

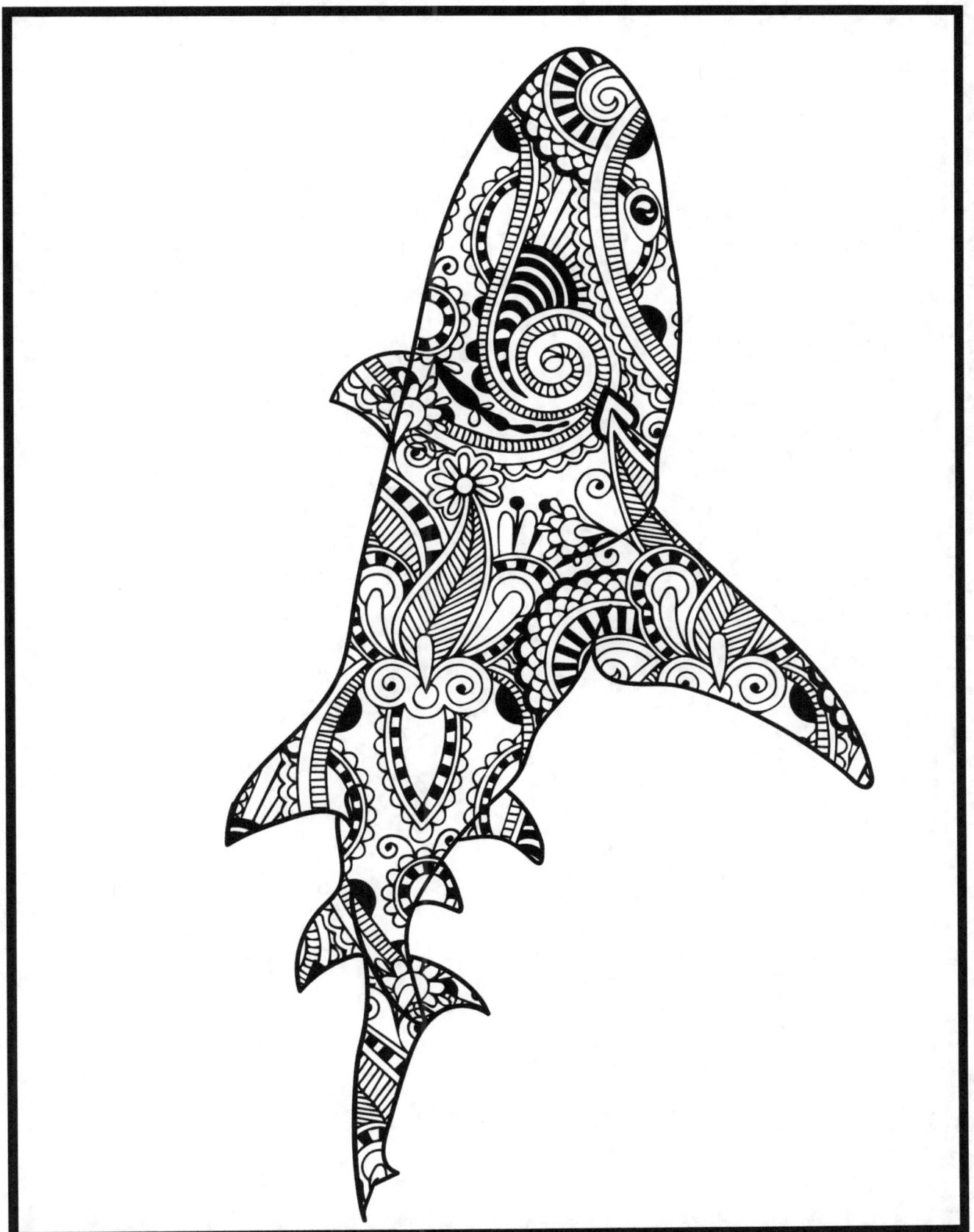

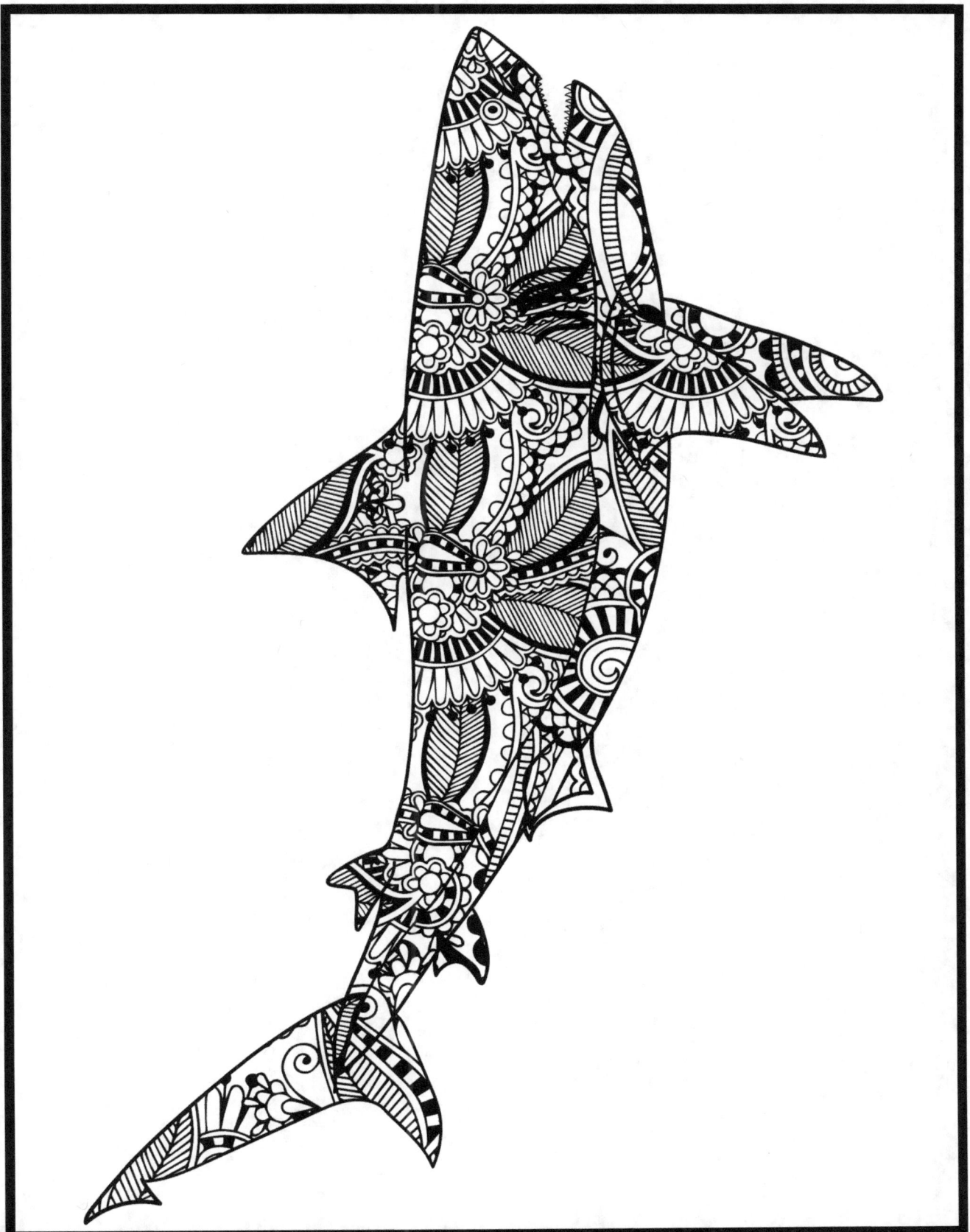

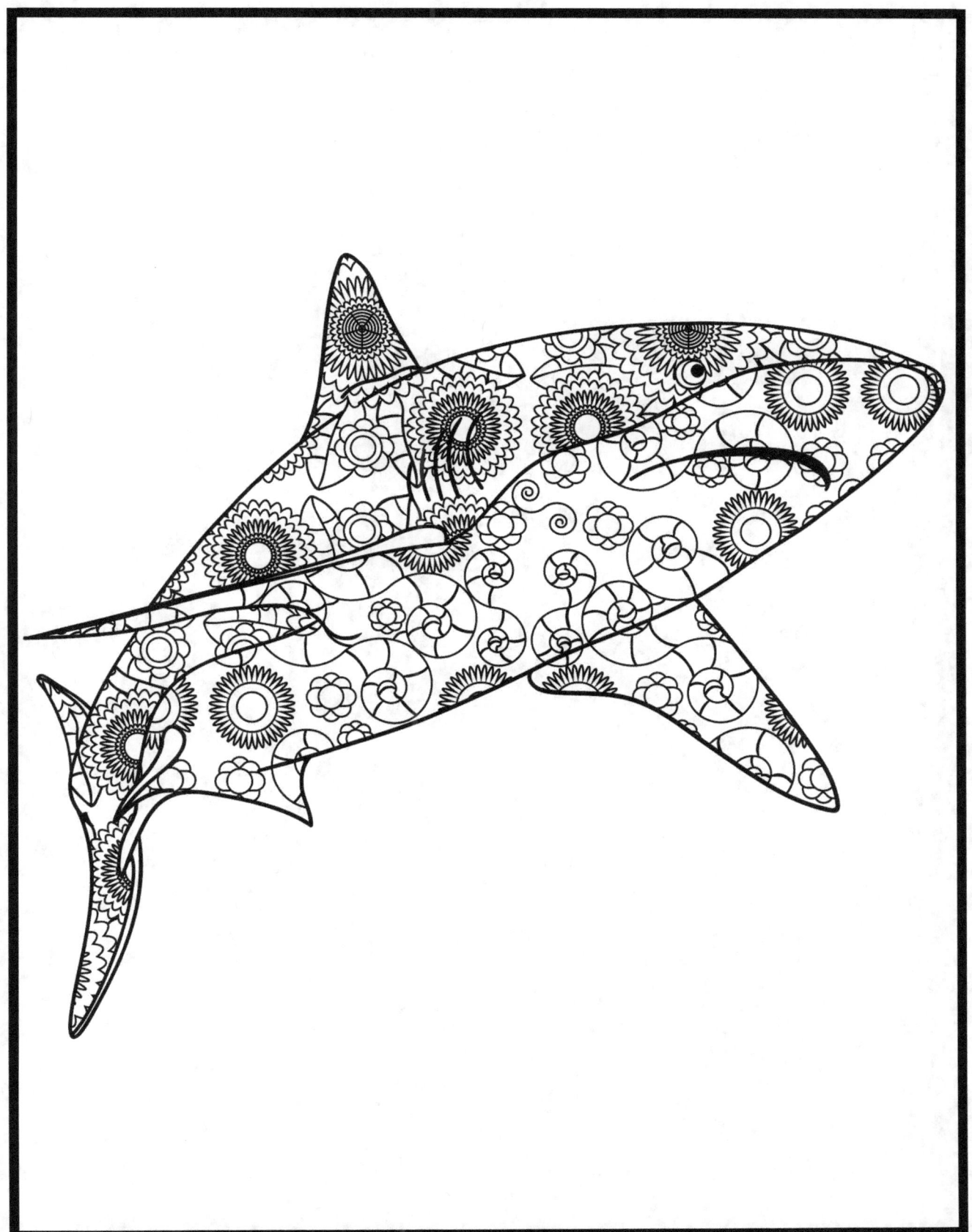

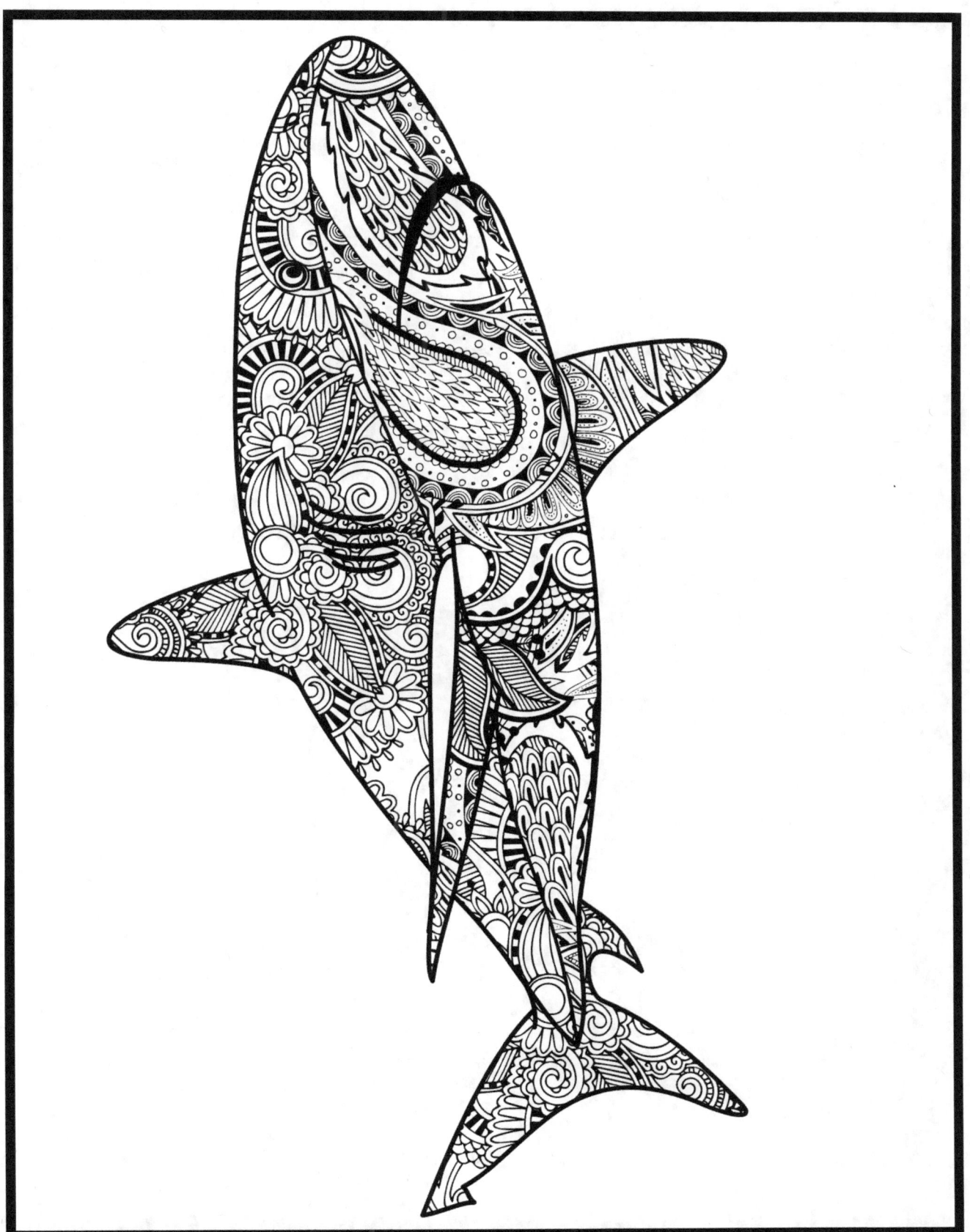

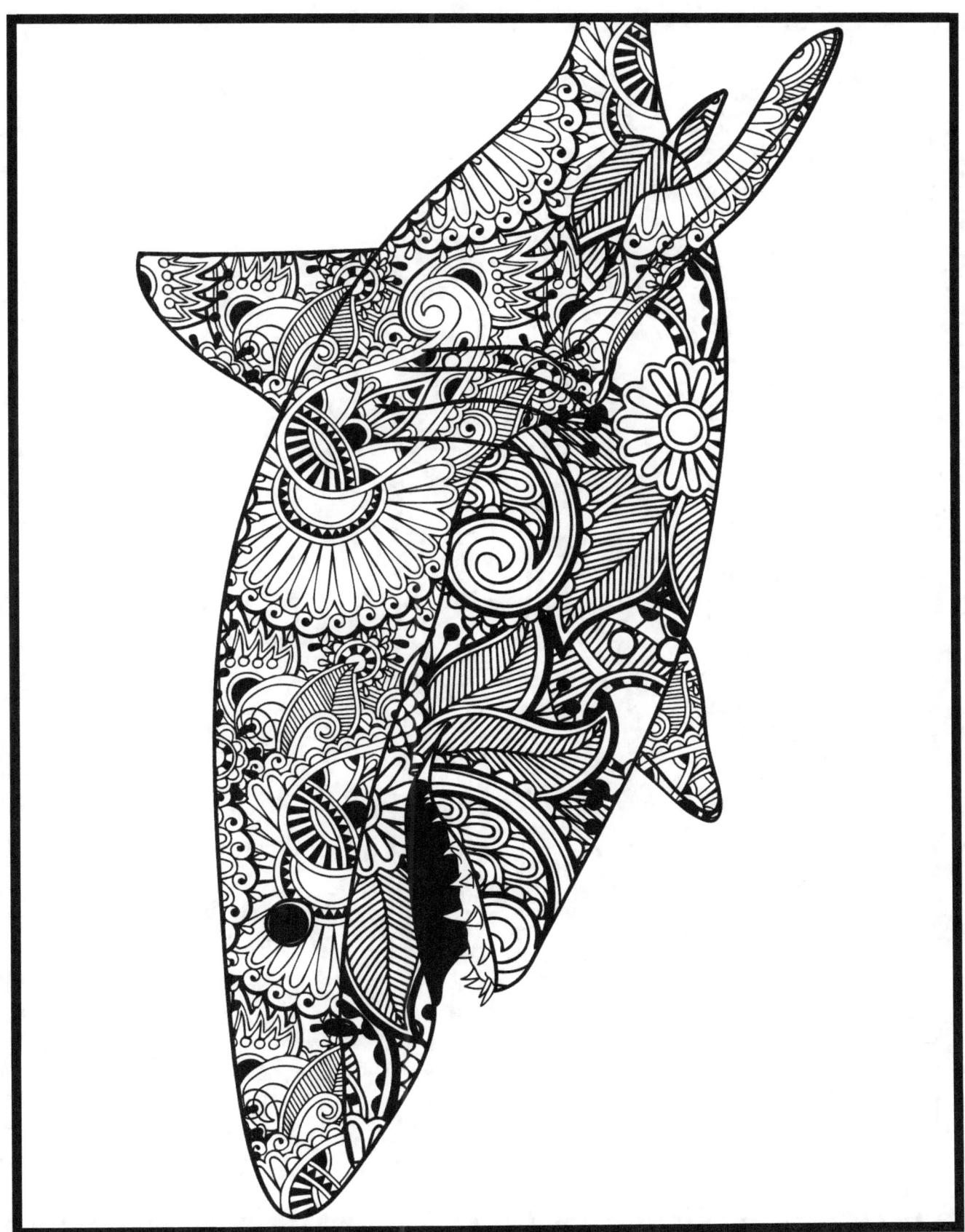

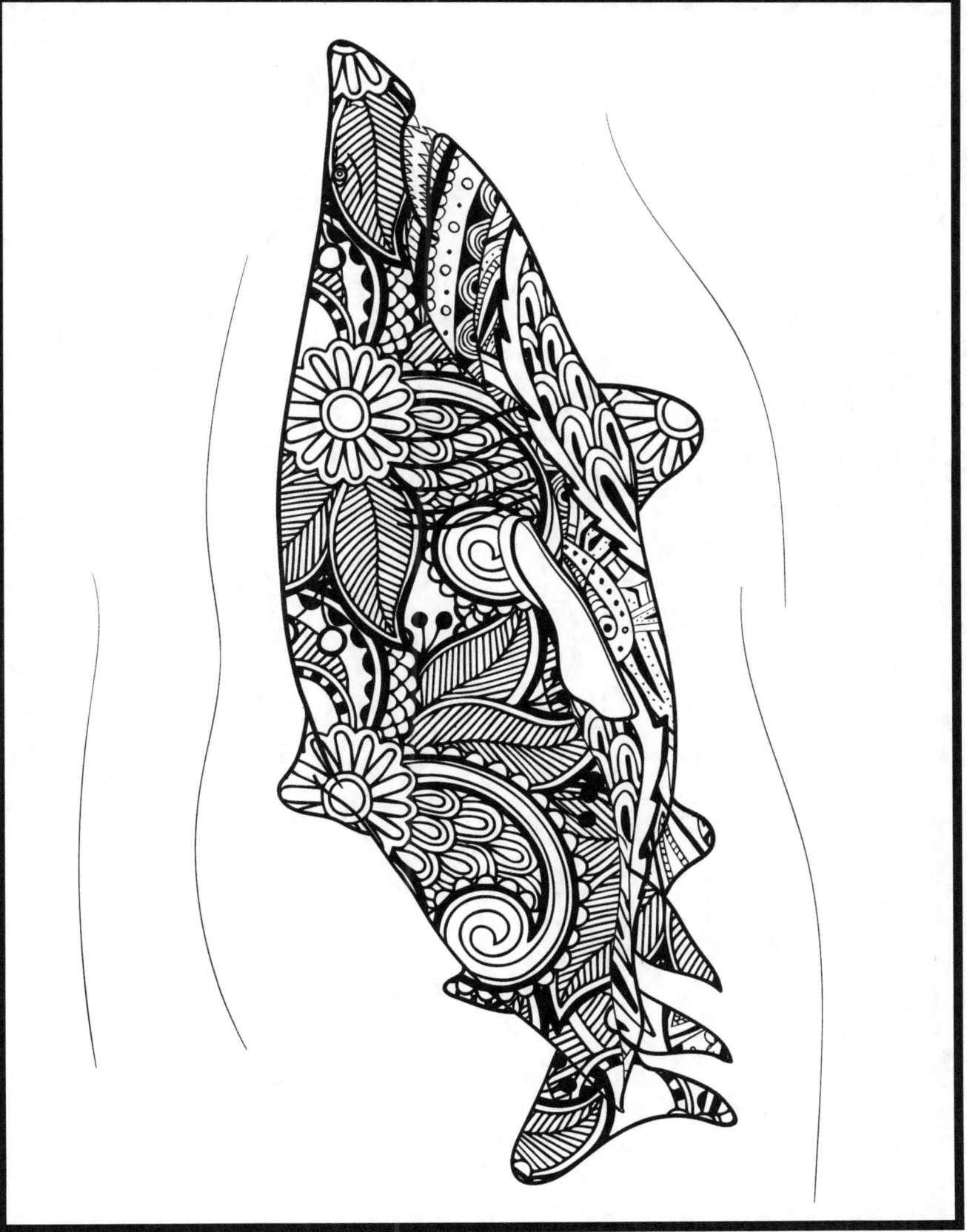

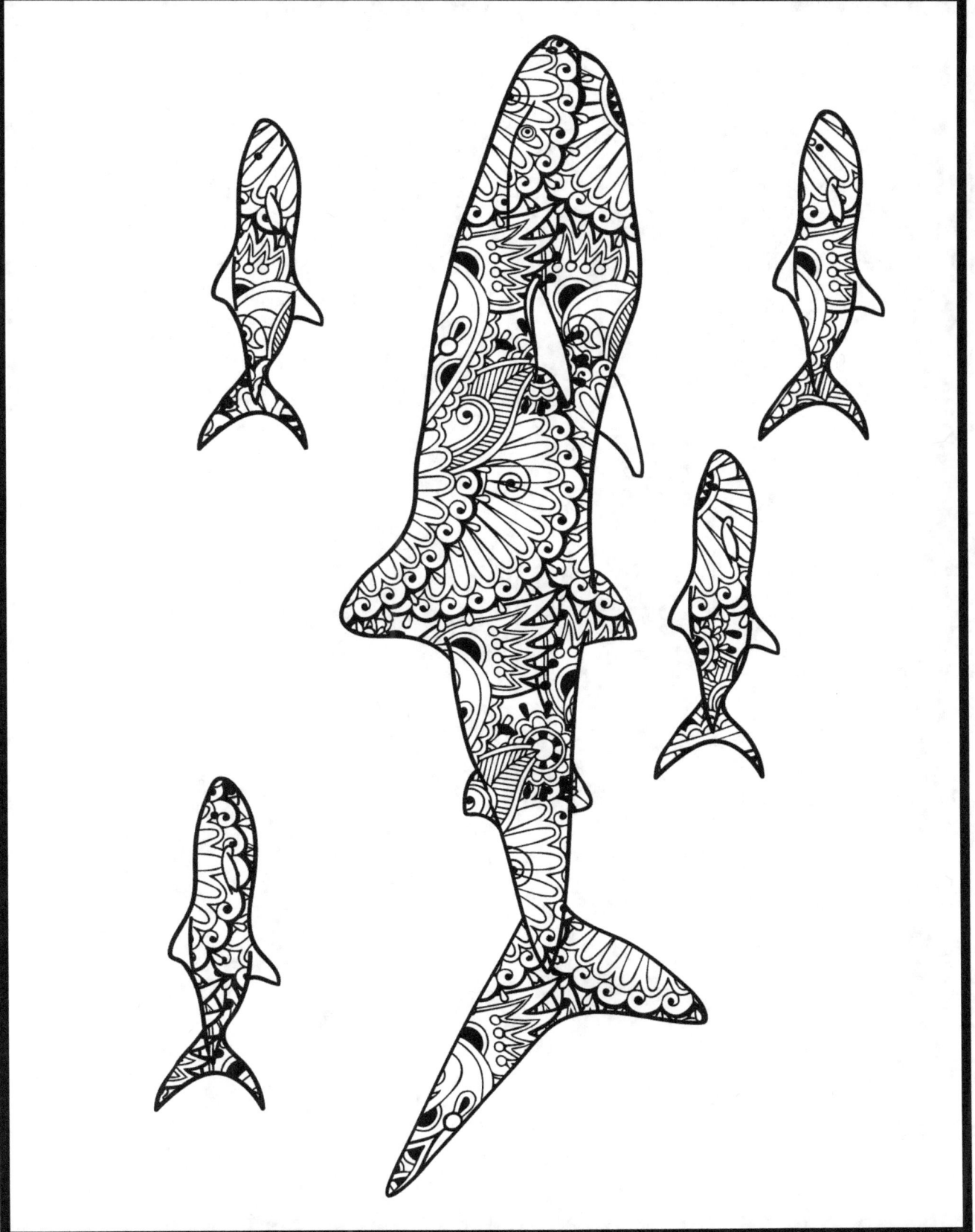

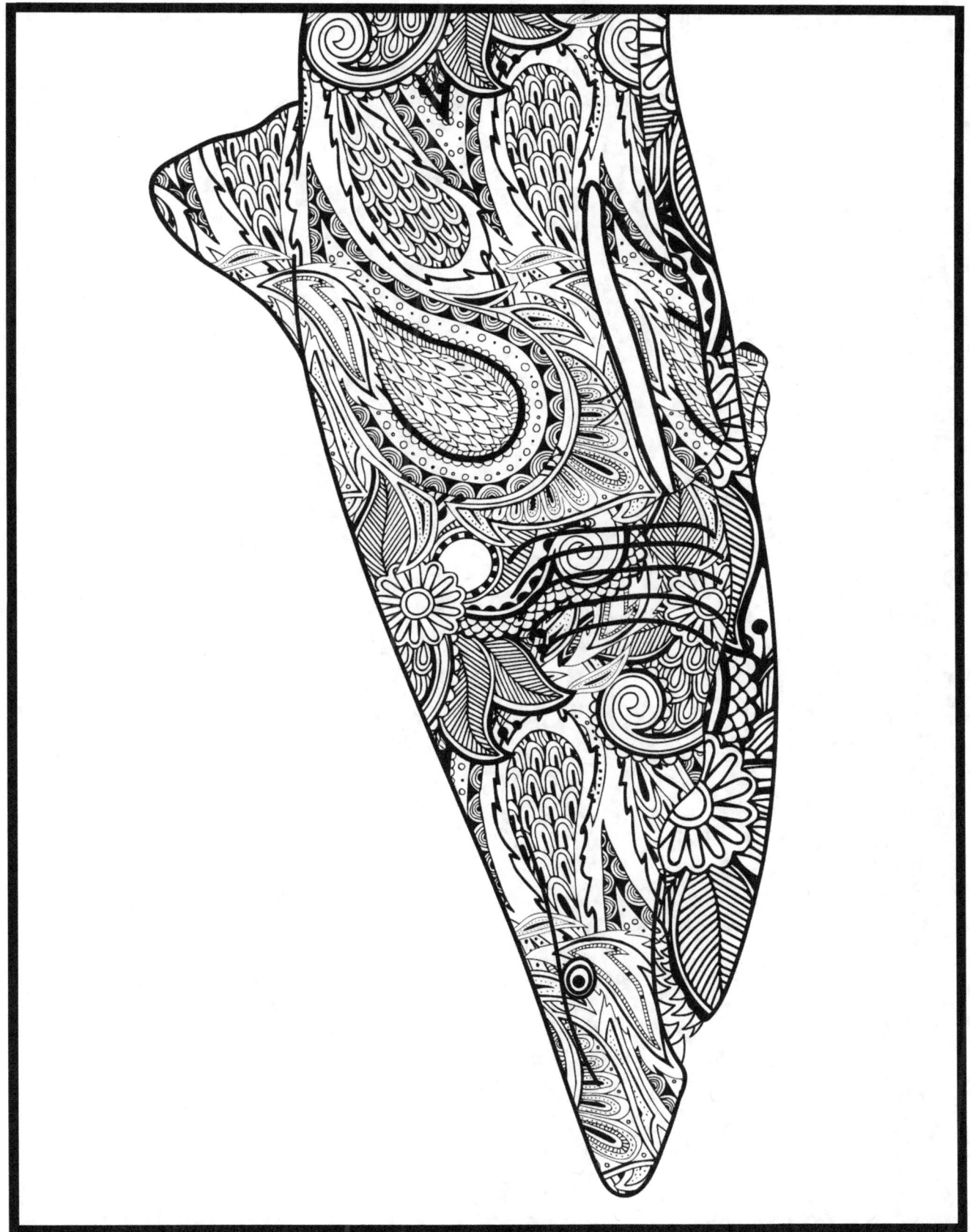

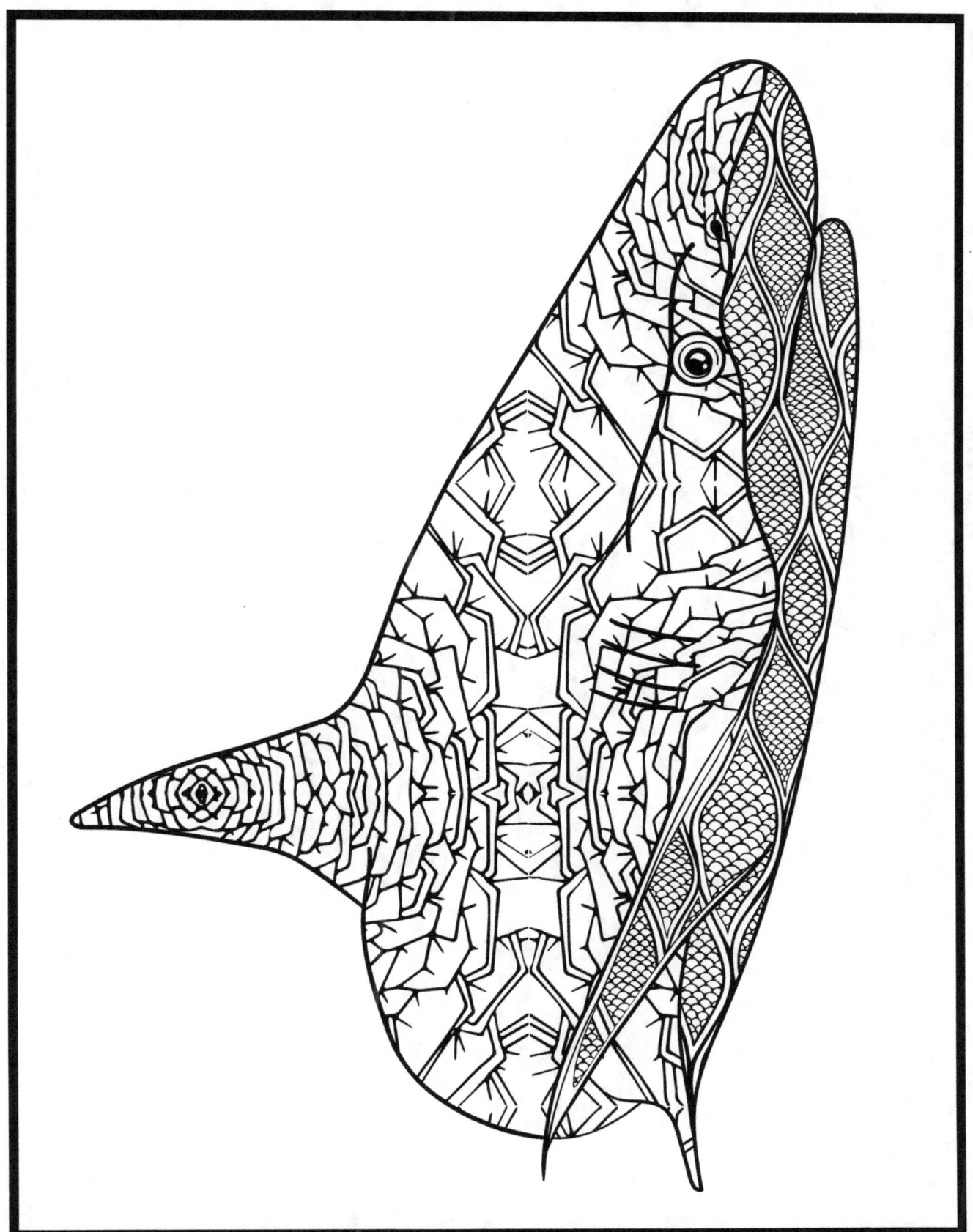

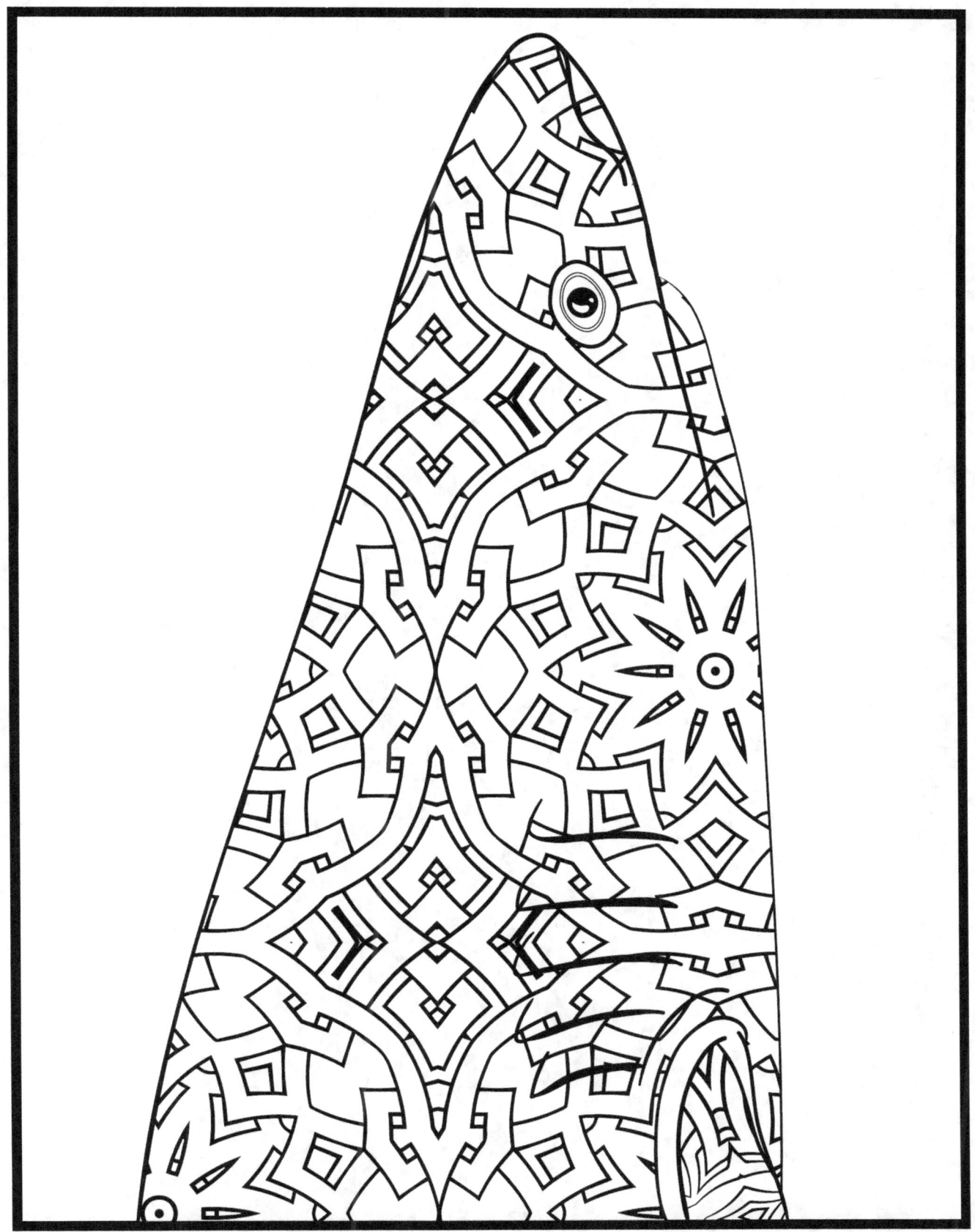

# COLOR TEST PAGE

# COLOR TEST PAGE